チュ…
チュ…

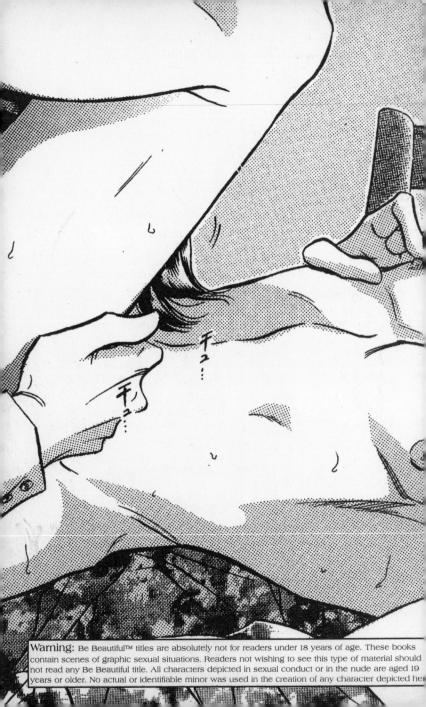

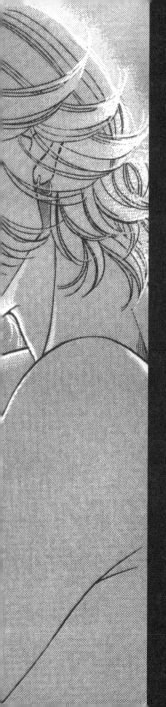

Melanie Schoen
Translation

RIN and Diana Brantuas
Retouch & Lettering

Evelyn Grand
Design

Michelle Locque
Director of Print Production

Mariko Kumanoya
Publisher

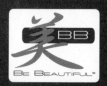

BeBeautifulManga.com

Embracing Love 4. Published by Be Beautiful™, an imprint of A18
Corporation. Office of Publication – 250 West 57th Street, Suite
328, New York, NY 10107. Original Japanese version "Haru wo
daiteita Volume 4" © 2001 Youka Nitta. Originally published in
Japan in 2001 by Diblos Co., Ltd. English version © 2006 A18
Corporation. Be Beautiful, Original Yaoi and logos are trademarks
of A18 Corporation. All rights reserved. Price per copy $15.99,
price in Canada may vary. Printed in Canada

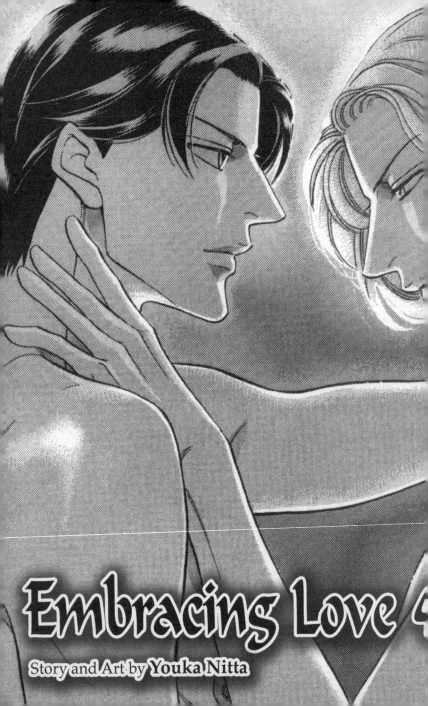

Embracing Love 4

Story and Art by **Youka Nitta**

CONTENTS

Profile:
KYOSUKE IWAKI

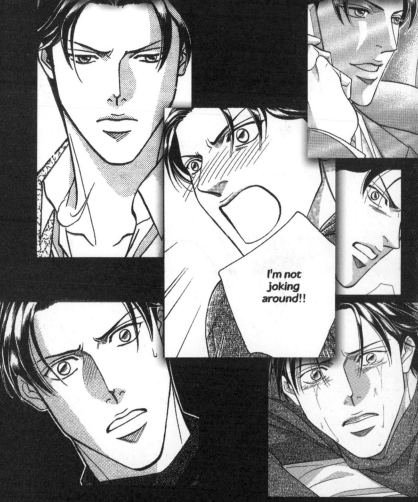

I'm not joking around!!

his ruggedly handsome adult film star's life was turned upside-down when he fell in love with his arch-rival, Katou. Is desperately trying to strike a balance between his relationship with Katou, his family and his career.

Character
YOJI KATOU

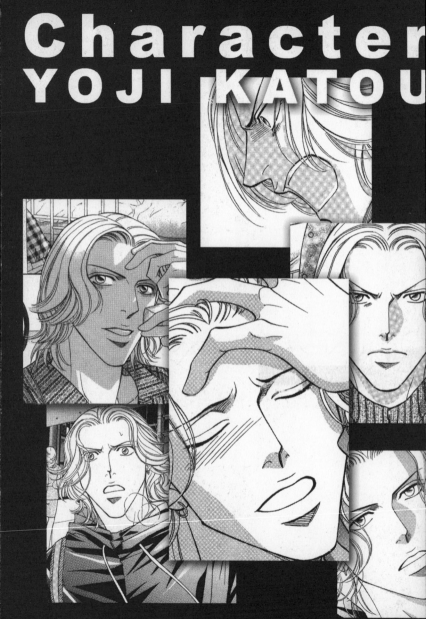

This beautiful blonde is Iwaki's opposite in every way. His passionate feelings for Iwaki know no bounds, and there's nothing he won't do to please his partner.

Profile:
NAGISA SAWA

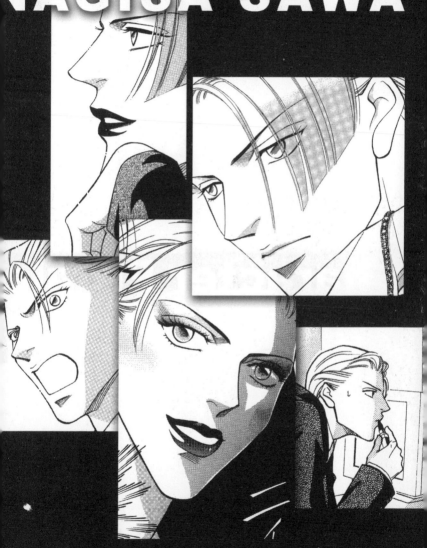

his author and director is as famous for creating the popular *Embracing ve* franchise as he is for his flamboyant crossdressing.

Character
MS. SHIMIZU

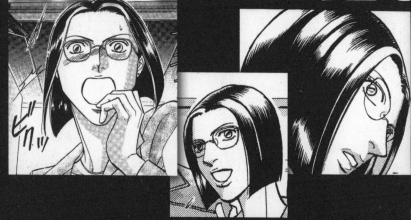

Iwaki's personal assistant will go above and beyond the call of duty.

Character Profile
YUKIHITO ASAK

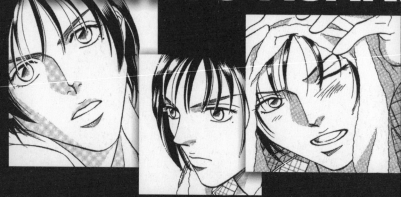

Sawa's lover and personal assistant may be shy on the outside, but it's what's on the inside that counts.

YOSUKE IWAKI, a popular adult film star, was pleased to audition for a film called *Embracing Love,* but he was shocked to discover that his arch-rival, the blonde and beautiful YOJI KATOU, was also up for the role.

After they shared a passionate sex scene (at the request of the director, the cross-dressing NAGISA SAWA), Iwaki won the part, as well as Katou's heart.

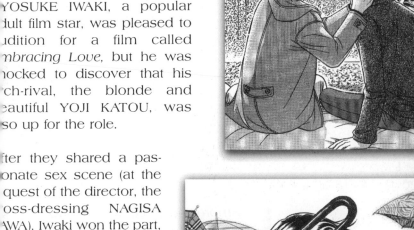

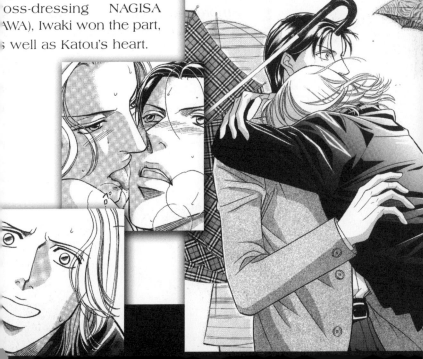

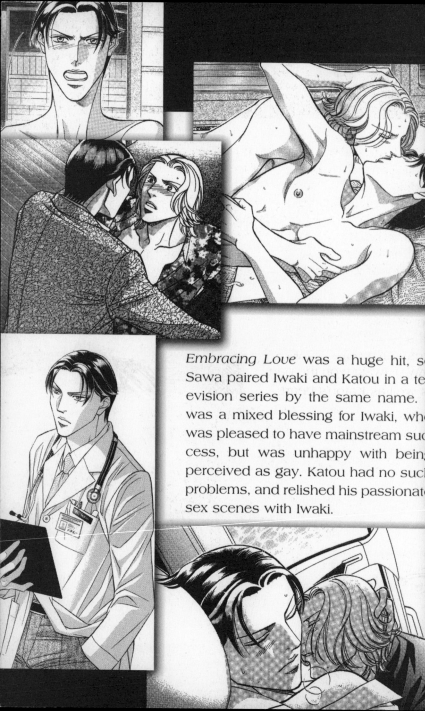

Embracing Love was a huge hit, s‹
Sawa paired Iwaki and Katou in a te‹
evision series by the same name.
was a mixed blessing for Iwaki, who
was pleased to have mainstream su‹
cess, but was unhappy with being
perceived as gay. Katou had no suc›
problems, and relished his passionate
sex scenes with Iwaki.

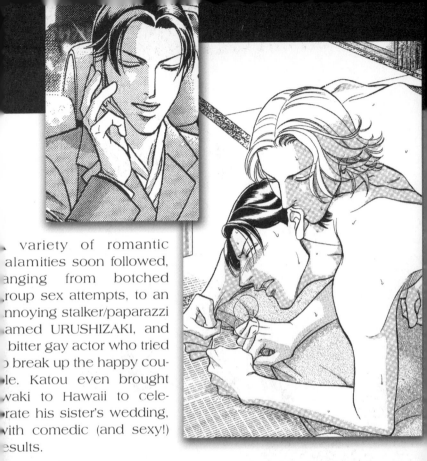

A variety of romantic calamities soon followed, ranging from botched group sex attempts, to an annoying stalker/paparazzi named URUSHIZAKI, and a bitter gay actor who tried to break up the happy couple. Katou even brought Iwaki to Hawaii to celebrate his sister's wedding, with comedic (and sexy!) results.

Things took a sour turn when Iwaki received tragic news: His mother had recently passed away. Iwaki returned home to his estranged family, and had multiple confrontations with his brother, MASAHIKO. Only through Katou's timely intervention was a tentative truce reached between the brothers.

Our heroes returned to their brand new home and decided to focus on their careers, which brings us to the latest chapter of our story...

Dr. Mitani
三谷良一

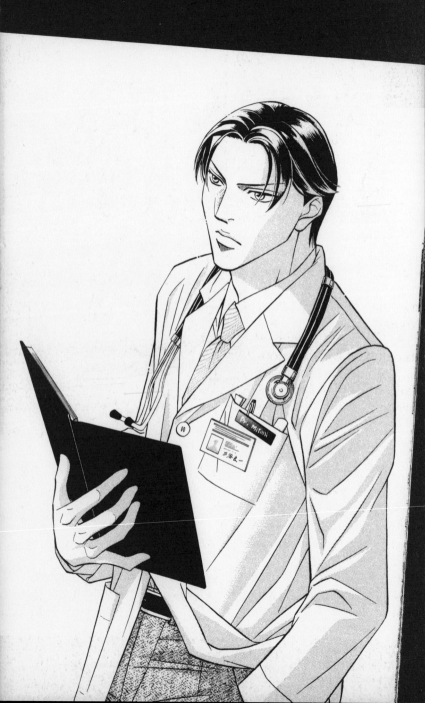

Hotel Okura
The New Otani
Thank you all of you for coming...
To the press conference for our **new program.**
インサイド・レポ
inside report
月10日(月)夜9:00スタート
TBS
Snap
Snap
her Best
ハーベスト
Starting Monday at 9:00 p.m.

ON)PM9:00
Best
テレビ
Mr. Yoji Katou You're being photographed with your lovely lady costars...
But wouldn't you **prefer** to have a certain handsome **gentleman** next to you?
DON
What!?
That has nothing to do with this. I'm **honored** to work alongside such fine ladies.
How about the new that your lover, **Mr. Kyosuke Iwa** is shooting a dram to be aired the **same day and time** as yours?
What do you think? Will you be battling for ratings?
What a question. You make it sound like the numbers will affect our relationship.
Hotel Okura
Snap
This is a ***suspense drama*** is about a doctor who performs a medical error.
It focuses on the inner life of the surgeon I play, ***Ryuichi Mitani,*** and his struggles with the contradictions of the medical world.
Snap

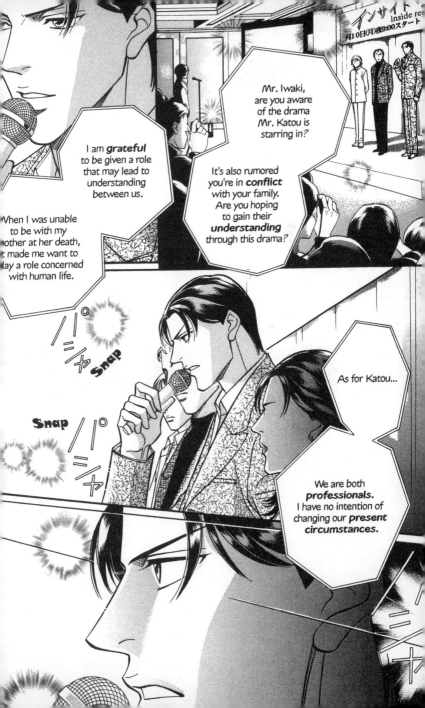

インサイト
inside re
月10日(月)夜9:00スタート

Mr. Iwaki, are you aware of the drama Mr. Katou is starring in?

I am **grateful** to be given a role that may lead to understanding between us.

It's also rumored you're in **conflict** with your family. Are you hoping to gain their **understanding** through this drama?

When I was unable to be with my mother at her death, it made me want to play a role concerned with human life.

Snap

Snap

As for Katou...

We are both **professionals.** I have no intention of changing our **present circumstances.**

CHATTER
CHATTER
As usual, another **serious comment** from Kyosuke Iwaki.
Is that bad? It **is** a serious drama.
Iwaki must have changed to be picked up for a show like this.
Perhaps he's just finally being recognized as a **real actor?** That couple must be earning a lot.
Katou's been in **how many** popular commercials by now?
Iwaki declares war on Katou
A war over ratings!
"I have no intention of interrupting my affairs."
BREAKING NEWS!
Expectations for both shows
her Best
Man, those two! Just when you think they've run out, they become even **more popular**.
"...the numbers wi affect our relationship...

Iwaki-san and I had strict schedules to begin with...
Because we both took time off so he could go home.
In the two weeks since then...
We've been under pressure again.
So of course, we haven't had any time...
To even see each other.

We're leaving now...
BEEP
No. Not home yet, after all.
Iwaki's running late?
That's **too bad**, since you ended **early** for once.
It's not that.
Even if he **were** home we'd just stare at each othe It's hard to talk t him lately.
月10日(月)夜9:00スタート
新番組
インサイド・レポート
inside report
SONY
That role... must be a **dream** for him.

Iwaki-san really **is** cool when he's on TV...
SIGH
But he's **cuter** when I hold him.
Hm?
Did you say something?
I was thinking that Iwaki-san should come work at **our** agency!
We could synchronize our days off... Have more **time together.**
It's nothing!

Ahh, I think our bosses would jump at it, if you told them.
But I don't think Iwaki would like it. He'd say "You can't mix business with your personal life!"
Whatever.
Now that I think of it, we've never really talked about that.
PAT
ぱた
But now that I think about it...
We haven't even seen each other for a week.
I wonder if Iwaki-san thinks about it at all.
That last press conference made it sound like a break up.

Press
Why don't you try **asking him** about switching agencies?
It'd be easier to coordinate off days together that way, right?
There are a **lot** of cases of actors taking the same agency after they're married.
...I don't think **that's** it.
It sounds like a good idea when you think of it **that way.**
Even Iwaki will have to think about it, coming from you.
Though you'd better not try and switch.
I want to see Iwaki-san...!

Stop the car!! I'm going to persuade him right now!!
SCREECH
Wha!?
ガチャ G-cha
Hey!! Katou!!
EEEH!
beep
beep
Hello. Shimizu!?

Tump!
Where is Iwaki-san working right now?
Click
He's at a photography studio in Midoriyama.
If you hurry you might still catch him.
Take me to Midoriyama Studio.
SHHHH
TBS
Midoriyama Studio

Studio 7
Studio 8
Inside Report
Studio 9

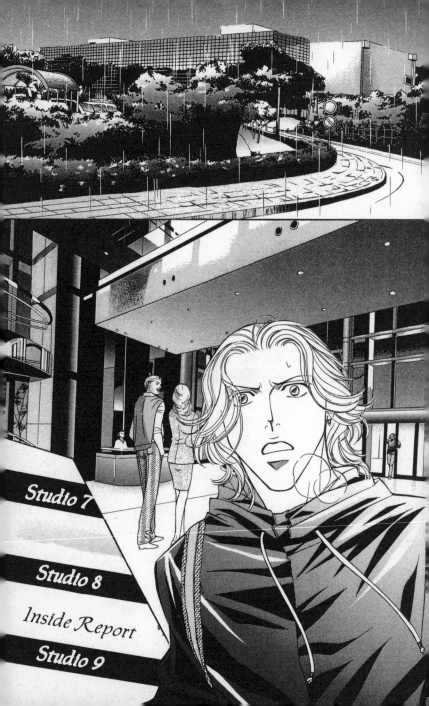

Studio 8
Huh? Katou?
Didn't Katou leave already?
Iwaki-san!!

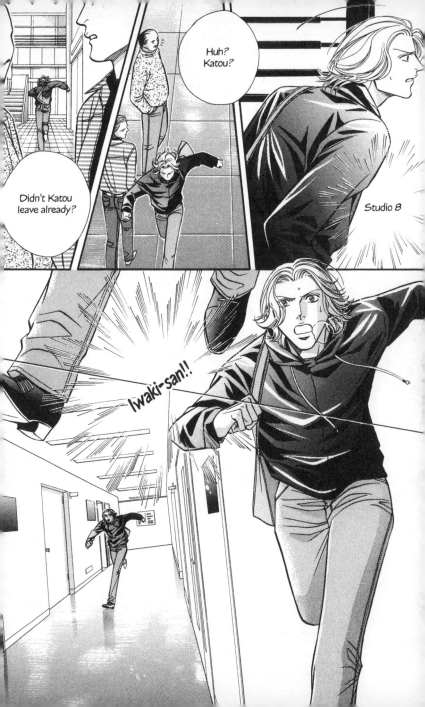

Huh? Iwaki?
He left a few minutes ago.
What!? No!

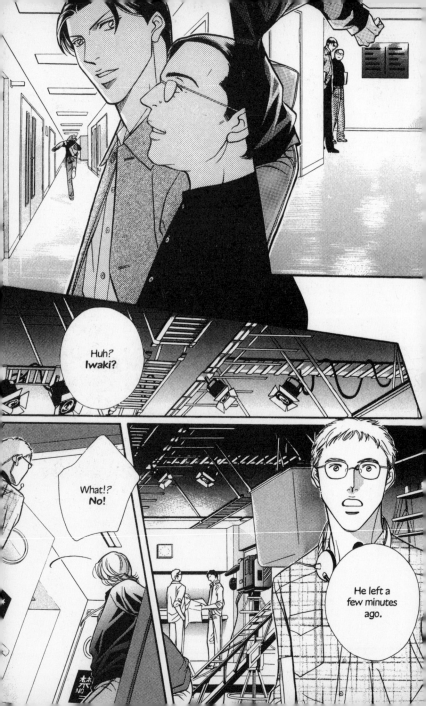

Iwaki-san!
You're driving home today, Iwaki? Where's your manager?
She wasn't feeling well, so I came in my own car.
Well, see you tomorrow.
Good work today.
Sigh
FWOOP

I was able to leave early today.
Drip
Drip
Drip
Katou's probably still working...
Iwaki-san!!

Katou?
Iwaki-san!!

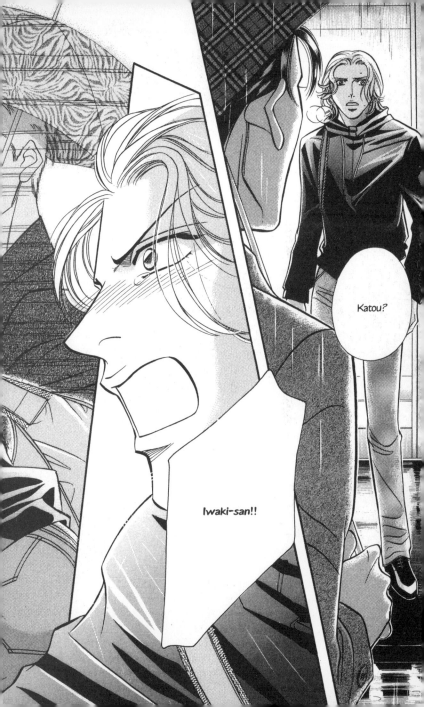

Iwaki-san!
Oh, Iwaki-san! How I've missed you!
You idiot, everyone's watching!!

Drip
Drip
Ahh...
Nnnn!

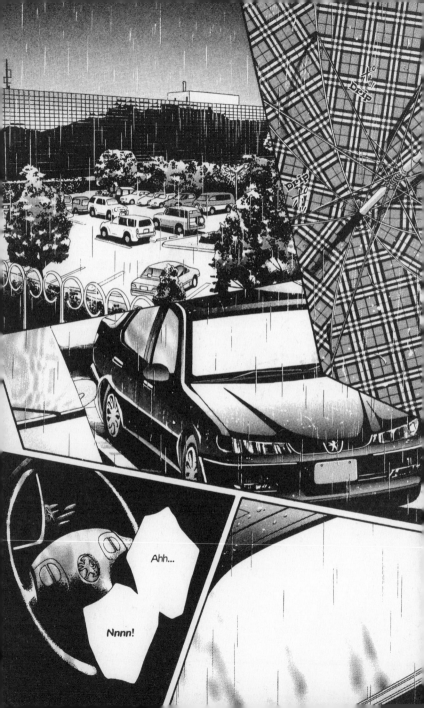

Can't you wait until we get home...?
Ohh, Katou...!!
No, I can't!!
You know how I feel, right!? We haven't seen each other for a whole week!!
Push
カチャカチャ
Zzzup!
I can't wait another second!!

What are you saying? It's just a week...
It's happened before.
Thrust
It's not just a week!
Aahh!
....
....
Ksssshhhh

Thap
Ah...!
Ah-ahhh!!
Thap
Thap
So, Iwaki-san...
You forgot **all about me** while you were doing your dream job?
Thap
Thap
I know we're busy with work...
But **this** is important too, isn't it?
Ah...
Ohh!!
Thap
At least you could've called me!!
sqikkk
Thap

Thap
Thap
Thap
Ahhh! Ahhh!
Ahhhhhh...!
Thap
I'm... coming...
Katou... I'm coming!!
TREMBLE
Ahh...!!

Haaaah
FLOP
Oh, Iwaki-san...
How I've missed you.
Kiss
SHHHHH

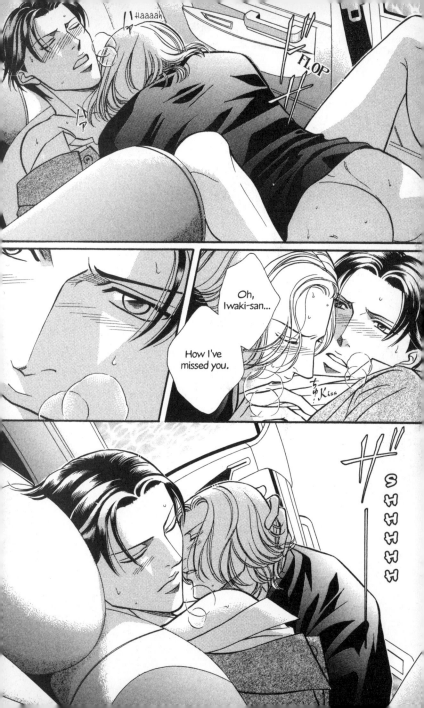

What should I do?
This would be a good time to ask him about changing his agency.
I have to think of **some** way to convince him.
Will he laugh... or get mad?
Um, Iwaki-san?

...Katou?
Huh!?
I didn't forget you for my work.
And to be fair, you've endured the same strict schedule.
I've been able to keep going because I knew you hadn't forgotten me.
If we couldn't see each other... I knew you'd still come to me like this.
You're the one that gave me that reassurance, Katou.

It's not fair, Iwaki-san. You always take every-thing on yourself.
But you're right. We **were** in the same position.
Even though we love each other, we couldn't be together.
...I hope we can be in **another** drama together someday.
I want to compete with **you**, not just your ratings.
Yeah... you're right.

But our love wasn't **so childish** that we had to spend every **moment** together.

The rain is stopping.

Yeah.

Are you all right Iwaki-san? Should I drive?

I'm all right. You must be tired, too.

By the way, I heard Shimizu wasn't feeling well.
Is she okay?
Vrrrm
She's pregnant.
She'll be taking maternity leave soon.
What!?
So you're getting a **new manager**!?
Well, yes.
K-chak
It's not some **handsome guy** ...Is it?

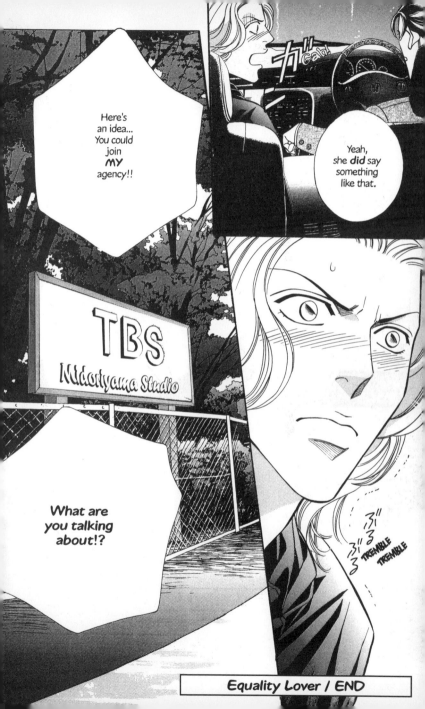

Here's an idea... You could join **MY** agency!!

Yeah, she **did** say something like that.

TBS
Midoriyama Studio

What are you talking about!?

TREMBLE TREMBLE

Equality Lover / END

クロス・ゲーム
CROSS GAME

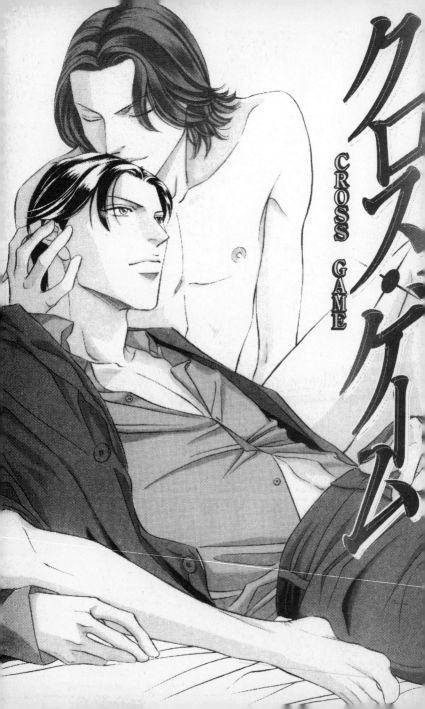

DING DONG
G-CHAK
Startle
Good morning-**Kyaaa**!!
Dah-Dumm!
Oh, Katou! You **surprised** me.
Good morning. Where's Iwaki?
I'm sorry, Shimizu. He's been like that all morning.
TAK
TOK

He's been in a bad mood since he heard I'm getting a new manager.
I hope it's all right that we popped over?
Hey, move so she can take her shoes off.
C'mon, Iwaki-san! What worries me is...!
I'm sorry. I worked hard until my absence so there **wouldn't** be any trouble.
See? Now you've made her **worry**!
No, it's not **you**, Shimizu!
I'm really glad you've had your baby.
TOK TOK
It's all right. I **understand**.
You were worried about Iwaki's work now that he has a **new manager**.

Shizumi, I parked the car at the corner. Is that all right?
Ah, just in time. I can introduce you to Katou, too.
This is **Nobuyuki Asano.** He will be taking over for me.
I'm Asano. It's a pleasure to be working for you, Iwaki-san.
!
You're so good-looking, Iwaki-san. More like an ***actor*** than a manager.

Yes. He was recently scouted by our agency, and we wanted to get him to work right away.
He doesn't know much about the acting world, so we thought he should make his debut after learning from you, Iwaki.
Nice to meet you, Iwaki-san... And thank you for this opportunity!
I promise you that I'll do my best.
All right then Asano, could you pull the car around?
Sure.

That little ...!
Flinch
Smile
Well, we're going.
You'd better get ready so you're not late.
Just a minute, Iwaki-san.
Take this.
A cell phone?
I bought it for you. It will hard for us to keep in touch without Shimizu.
I already programmed my number in, in case something happens.

Idiot. What could happen?
Well, I'm leaving.
See you later.
What are you looking at?

Nothing.
I was just thinking, you two really get along.
That's right. We're *totally* in love. And I won't let you get away with causing him any trouble.
Smile
I'll do my best.

TBS
Midoriyama Studio
Okay, cut!
Please check the monitor!

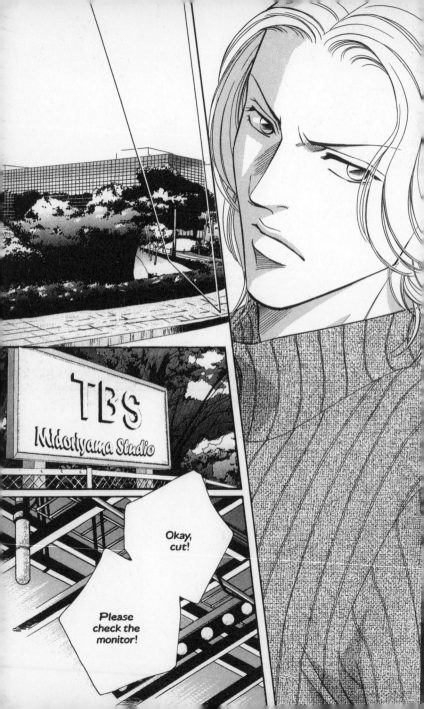

RING
RING
RING
RING
Hm?
Someone, get that phone! We're recording!

Whose is it?
Mutter
Mutter
Huh?
Isn't that **Iwaki's phone!?**
I'm sorry! **It's my phone!**
I'm sorry for interrupting!!
I'm sorry. It's his **first day** today.
What an **idiot**! Doesn't he have any idea how **expensive** this shoot is? Time is money! If we need to re-shoot that, I'll...
HUH?
Wait, was that...?

I'm sorry, Asano-kun!!
I'm sorry, Asano. **Thank you.**
Not at all. It's my job to cover for Iwaki-san... **No matter what!**
I'll just turn it off for good measure.
RUSTLE

BLINK
Message received.
BEEP

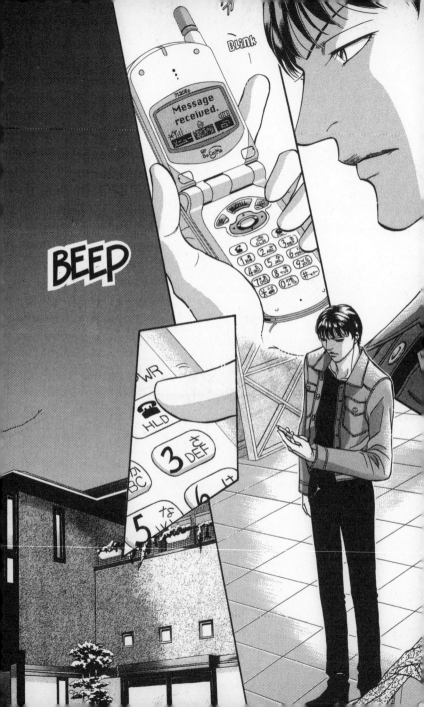

SLIP
I'm really not very good with those things.
I forgot to turn the sound off, so when it rang during shooting I didn't realize it was mine.
If Asano-kun hadn't been sharp enough to take the blame, I would've really **lost face.**
SLIDE
I think he's going to work out **just fine.**
.....
SLURP
CLATTER
Thanks for dinner!

CLANG
What's with your attitude, Katou?
What!? **Excuse me** for giving you a phone!!

What, are you upset over **that?**
Wasn't I **laughing** about it just now? It's **my fault** I forgot to turn off the sound.
How thick can you **be,** Iwaki-san!?
GRIP
I **don't** want to hear you talk about **other men** when **you're with me**!
Can't you think about **my** feelings!?

What's with t
hysterics? W
always tal
about work
And don't say "other men." Why are you overreacting like this?
Shimizu and I were always together, but you liked her, too. Now things are changing because he's a guy?
Think about poor Asano-kun! He totally took the blame for me!
It's not because he's a guy... It's because I'm a guy!
I'd never loved another man before, but now I love you so much!!
How can you say no other man could feel the same!?
And besides, I have the feeling that... That he's trying to take you away from me!!

You're acting strange today. Just cool your head.
You always strust me. If 're so "in love" t you can't see aight anymore, it's over.
Well, isn't that great for you!
It's because I'm so in love that you can be so calm!

Don't tell yourself I'll be fine if you don't do anything for me...
What!?
I want to be reassured that **you** want me, **too**!!
Just recently, you said you were able to do you work because of the reassurance **I** give you.
That's right! I **always** chase after you! All **you** do is wait!

I want you to want me more!!
...!

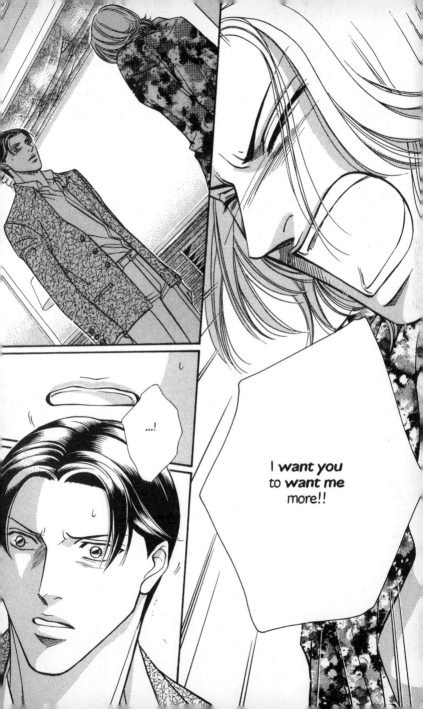

You mean...
My feelings aren't reaching you?
No...I'm sorry. I know I shouldn't be saying this.
I know you and I have **different ways** of loving someone!
And yet...
I still get uneasy. Sometimes I think we're **too happy** for it to **not fall apart!**

That's why...
I'm scared that something will change. I want to stay like this forever!
Katou...!!

I'm sorry. I let you sp me...Witho considering your feelin
Sometimes I forget that I'm older than you.
I'm sorry too, Iwaki-san. I'll only be this pathetic today.
Forgive m...!
Eee... Nnn...
Mm...Iwaki... san...
RUSTLE

Iwaki-san?
A long time ago you told me...
About the joy of being made love to by someone you care about.
I've tasted it *so many* times...
RUSTLE
Now...I'll show *you*...

KISS
...N
FLINCH
Ah...?
Ahh...
Iwaki-
san...!

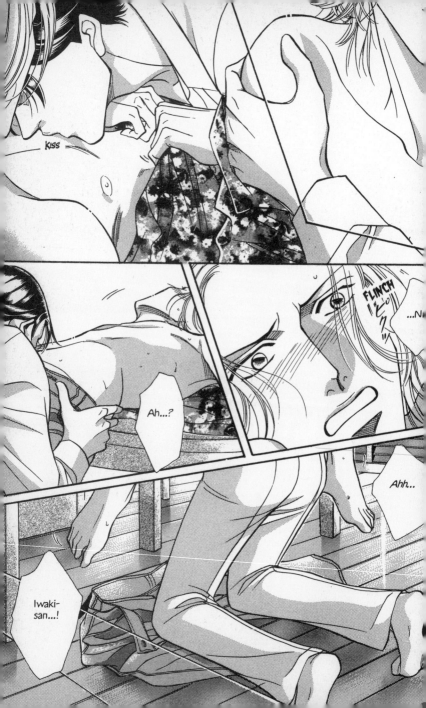

...!!
FLINCH
KISS
HFFF!
HFFF!
Nn...
Haa...
What's wrong? You don't have to stay so quiet.
know... But...

What are **you** embarrassed about? You **always** do this to me.
Is this **really** how you feel when I touch you?
Hff
Hff
When your lips and hands touch me... I'm so happy... I could cry.
TH-THUMP

Why are you talking so cute now?
You're the one...
That filled me with that happiness.
All right?
Yeah...
Katou?
Yes?

I should tell it's been a since I've ta anyone.
Don't be mad if I'm not **enough** for you.
That's right.
You've only been with **me** all this time.
Somedo
THRUST
Uhn...
Someday...
It doesn't have to be now...
Aaah...!!

I want this serious Iwaki-san...
hen I ake im...
To make love to me...
Yesss!

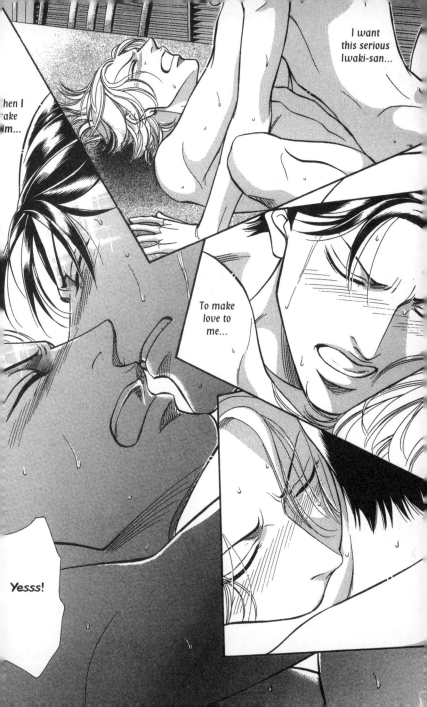

This is...a little embarrassing.
Yeah.

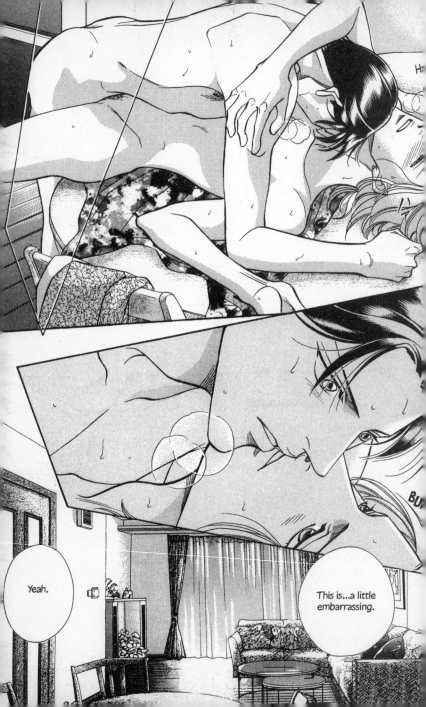

LIP
It's not connected...it's not getting a signal.
Did you turn it off?
Do you know how many times I tried calling?
No, I **don't** know.
Did Asano turn it off?
That's ridiculous. He wouldn't have taken such a liberty.
le would've st turned off the ringer.

What, are you **still** unsatisfied? I wasn't enough for you?
Iwaki-san...
Interpro
This is my desk, but I don't use it much.
You can use it while I'm on maternity leave.
Here are all the studio locations and contact information you need.

That's everything. Are you ready to start taking on more detailed work tomorrow?
Yes. Thank you.
Well, shall we walk down together?
ctually, I've got much to learn think I'll get started right now.
Good luck, then. Good night.
レコード会社
ファイル3
ファイル2
ファイル1
マスコミ関係名刺1
Media Contact Black List
マスコミ関係ブラックリスト

RING
ADDRES BOOK
RING
Hello?
Is this Mr. Kasai, the cameraman?
I've got some interesting news for you.
Who is this?
Have you heard the suspicious rumor about Kyosuke Iwak and his new manager?
Really!? That's...
BEEP

Yoji Katou got big after his scandal with Iwaki.
Let's see if the same thing will work for me. After all, you gotta do what you gotta do to get noticed.
No matter how I laughed off the phone business as my imagination...
I really didn't remember having turned it off.
Cross Game/END

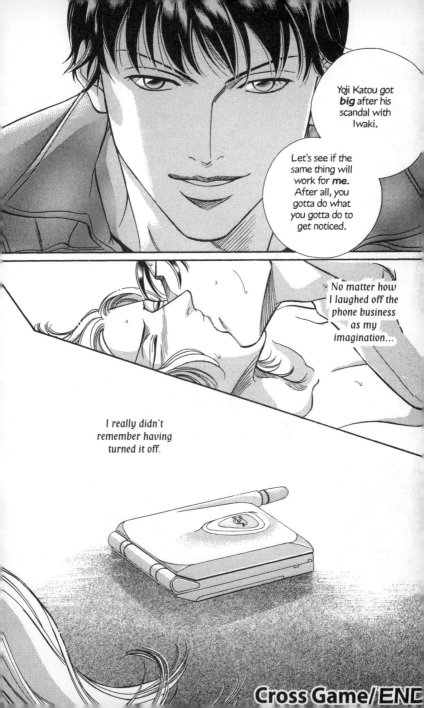

Inside Report
Oh, there you are, Komura. We're starting your interferon treatment today.
Oh no, Doctor...

ンサイド・
レポート
INSIDE REPOR

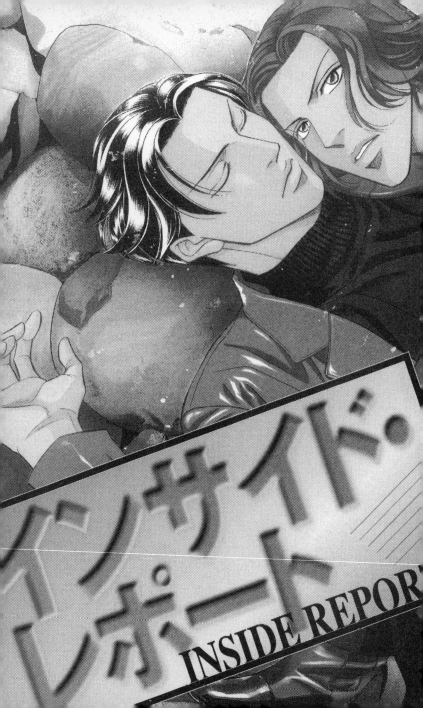

That stuff always makes me sick.
So you're running away? This is to help **cure you.**
Easy for **you** to say. **You've** never been shot with it.
Besides, even **with** all the pain it's still not a 100% cure.
FLIP
I starred in the drama Inside Report.
As the season was coming to a close, it became important to have a powerful advancement in the story.
FLIP
IWAKI
Casting the patient that would die as a result of the medical error was a huge struggle.

TBS
Midoriyama Studio
TOK
TOK
I understand the issue. He's the best, of course.
But Katou is the lead in the program **opposite** ours. There's **no way** they'll say yes.
We won't get a busy actor like **him** in the last month of shooting.
NO SMOKING
Yes, I'll try feeling them out.
Yes, we have other candidates. Yes, goodbye.

Good morning.
I couldn't help overhearing... You were talking about Katou?
Ah, good morning, Iwaki.
It's that screenwriter!
He says he wants Katou to play the patient.
Katou!? But that's impossible.
Didn't they want a **new face** for that role?
Yeah, but it seems that the screenwriter made the role with Katou in mind.
He doesn't like ***any*** of our candidates.
It's a ***small*** role, but it's important.
Iwaki, do you think you could talk to Katou about it?
Glance
ちら
HMPH.

CAUTION
I don't mix business with my personal life.
I knew it!!
What about **him?**
Doesn't he want to be an actor?
Yeah, I think he said something about wanting to act.
Well, Asano-kun? Will you audition?
Don't worry about **me.** I can get another manager.
It's your chance, right?

I appreciate your offer, but I would prefer not to...
Until after I've learned all I can from Iwaki-san.
Sorry, he's pretty serious about this.
No, no! That's even better! Very refreshing!
But if we can't get Katou, please reconsider!
I know we won't get him.
Yes.
Thank you very much.

Huh? I took it.
It's a **guest appearance,** right?
Co-starring together before a scandal... How **"realistic."**
What!?
SLAM!
What were you thinking!?

Don't mix wor...!
"Work with our private life!!"
Right?
I thought you'd say that.
If you knew that, then why...!?
ギッ
PUSH
If you must know...
I didn't agree to do it just to work with you.

My agency against it at until I convin them...
My appearance would pull in a huge audience! There's nothing to lose.
And I'm **not** such a coward that I'd turn down a chance to wear down the boundaries between us.
Okay, cut!!

Good work!
Next is the scene with Iwaki in the director's office!
Katou, you can wait here until your next scene, so take a break.
STAND
Okay! Thank you!
Kaneko, can you get my coat and a drink please?

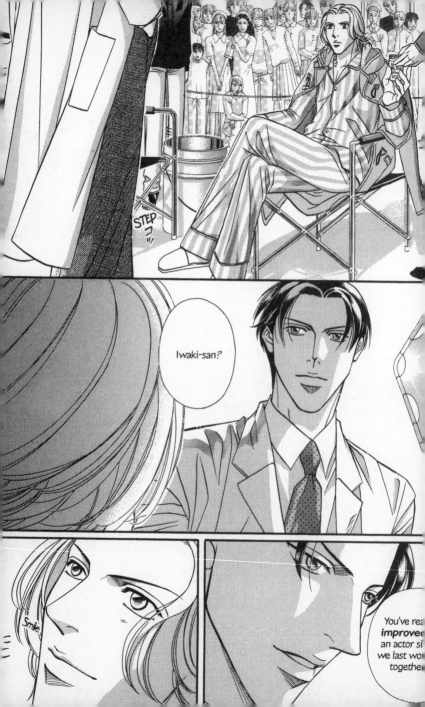

STEP

Iwaki-san?

Smile

You've rea
improve
an actor si
we last wo
togethe

You too, Iwaki-san.

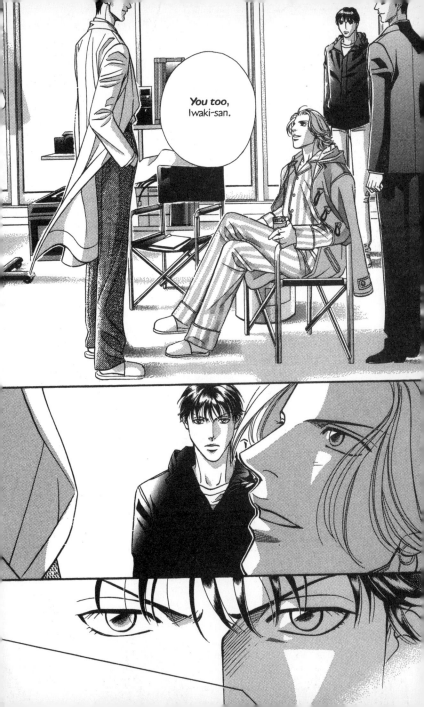

Are you saying we should HIDE that he got the infection from THIS hospital from his family!?
Komura's antibodies are fine!!
I have to tell his family that!! It can't be hepatitis!!
We must admit the **truth** to Koumura while he's still alive!!

No patient wants to hear that they weren't supposed to die.
A hospital isn't a charity, Dr. Mitani. **It's a business.**
If we lose our patients' trust, they'll stop coming, and everything will be over! A chief doctor like you ***should know that.***
Conceal the truth. **For everyone's sake.**

7
DING
6
5
You really portrayed the **duty** of a doctor vs. self-protection **very well.**
Next is Mitani's confession scene. Be sure to project his anger for his dishonest hospital.
And after that, he has to make **another** choice just before Katou's death.
"**Katou's death**"!? Please use the role's proper name!!
Sorry. I meant **Komura.**
No reason to overreact.

Katou is standing by. He doesn't look so good, though.
-THUMP
ドキ
Hi, Iwaki-san.

You look so pale.
I'm yellow, **and** black and blue. It sucks.
Take a good look, because I don't like to be seen when I don't look my best.
Idiot.
All right, start in five seconds!
Five...Four... ***three...!***

BEEP
Junya!!
BEEP
Hold on, Junya!!
Doctor!! Why is this happening!!
BEEP
SHUUU
BEEP
You said his condition was **improving**!!
BEEP

...?
FLIP
This is where he's supposed to rip off his lab coat in anger!
Camera Two! Close up on Iwaki!
Hurry!!

ピ

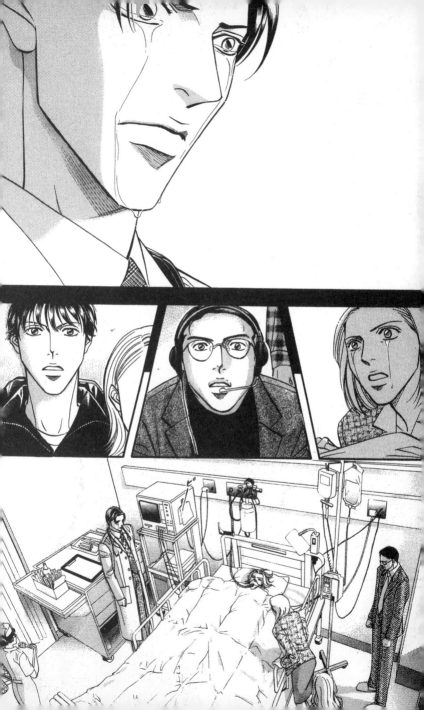

HAA!
Okay...CUT!!
Clap
Clap
Clap
I'm sorry, I... I wasn't paying attention.
Clap
Clap
Clap
That was **great**, Iwaki!
It was different from the script, but **very moving**!!
It **was**!?

Wipe your eyes, Iwaki-san.
You shouldn't cry in public.
What...!?

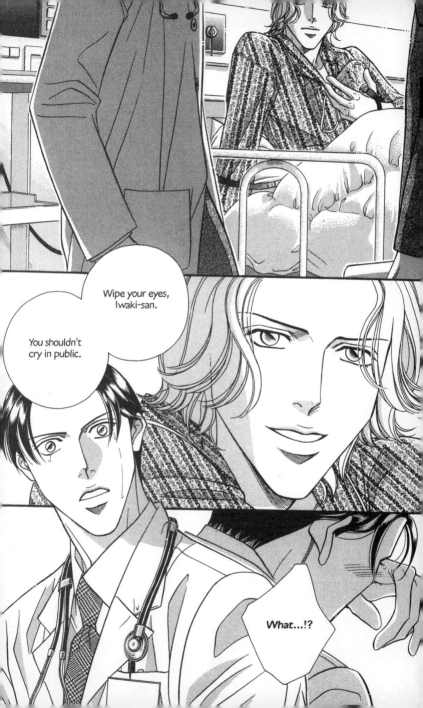

Iwaki-san?
Iwaki-san!!
HUH?
Oh! Sorry, Asano-kun.

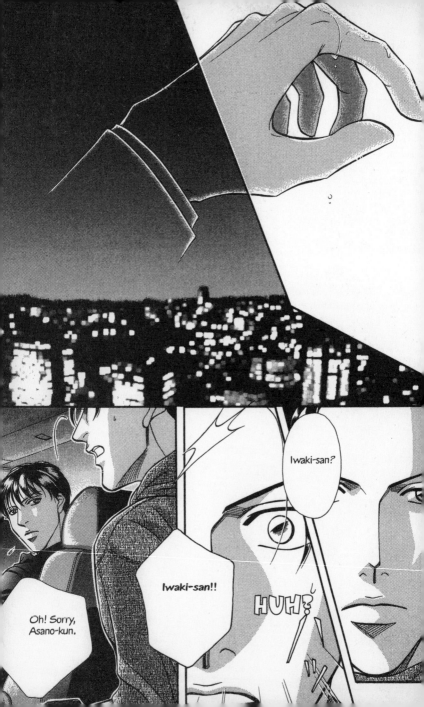

We're here.
K-CHAK
カチャ
Ah. Thanks.
By the way, I'm sorry you lost your chance to act.
Not at all.
wouldn't have een able to pull ch an amazing performance from you.
Whirrr

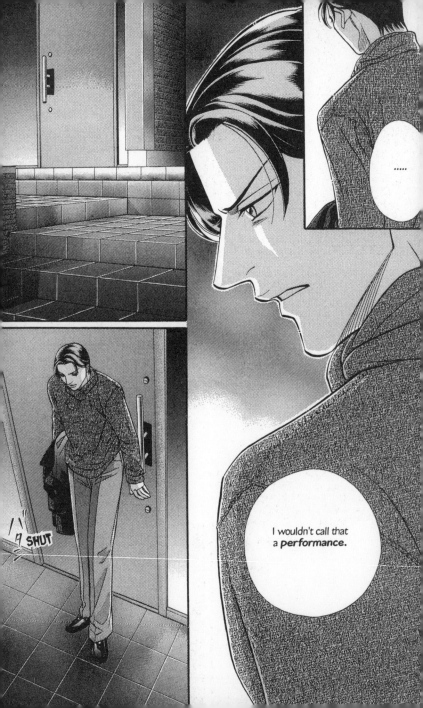

.....

SHUT

I wouldn't call that a *performance*.

TREMBLE

CLATTE
ガコ ガコッ
TMP
ダッ TMP
ダッ TMP
G-CHAK
RUSTLE
FFFUMP

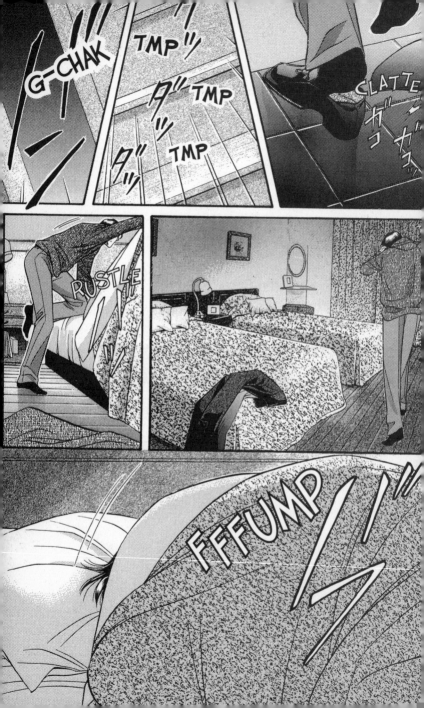

Katou...
CHIRP
CHIRP
Mnnnn...!

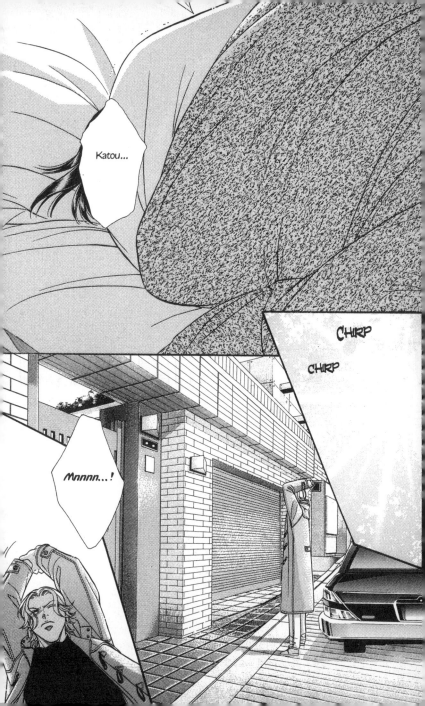

Great w last nigh can't bel it's morr alread
Fortunately we're done with the **night shoots.** I'll be back to pick you up at **three,** so get some rest.
Thanks, Kaneko. I'll be glad when our schedule is back to normal. See you later, then...
G-chak
ガチャ

He just...left his shoes scattered out?
He's never done that before.
Iwaki-san!?
TOK
TOK
Iwaki-san!?
TOK
SLAM

Iwaki-sa
What's wrong, Iwaki-san!? Are you sick!?
What happened?!?
YANK
Iwaki-san!!

Huh?
Why...Why are you...?

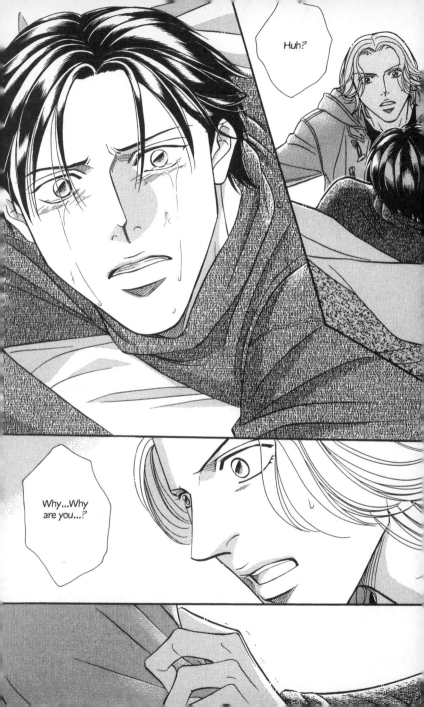

Katou.
Sigh
Iwaki-san...
So? What happened?

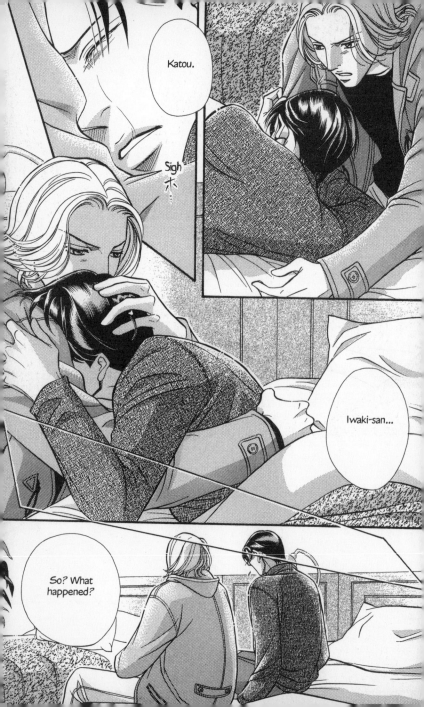

Asano didn't do anything to you, did he?
Why do you think it has to do with **him**!?
.....
SAG
I was scared that you'd come to **haunt me**!!
What's **that** mean?
You can't kill me off ***that easily.***

Besides, why're you scared?
You should be **happy** if someone you love comes back to **haunt you.**
You idiot!
To haunt someone you have to be **dead**!!
Do you know how I would feel...
If something happened to you while I **wasn't** with you?

Do you know how scared I was just **thinking** about you leaving me?
What would I do **all alone** in this house we built together?
I felt so cold watching you die in that scene.
I **never** want to feel that way again!!

Why are you so adorable?
It's just **too much** for me. I can't take it.
I'm not joking around!!
I know you're not.

Think about it. Could I really leave someone...
As cute as you all alone?
I'm not so dumb as to let anyone else have a chance at my Iwaki-san.

Mmm...
Hmm...
Haa...
Mnnn!
FLOP
ドサ
And besides...

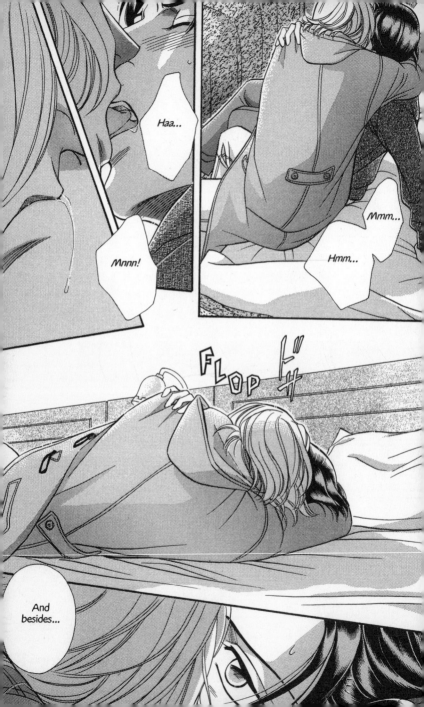

...I **already saw** how much you'd cry if I died.
I can't die if it meant seeing that again.
Stop talking about death! It's bad luck.
Heh.
PUSH
You were tossing it around just now.

You're working **so much.** Don't you need to rest?
Yeah, but I don't want to waste our time together, either.
I know it's been hard on you, Iwaki-san...
But I'm really glad I took this job.
You never talk about *Inside Report*, so I finally got to learn about it.

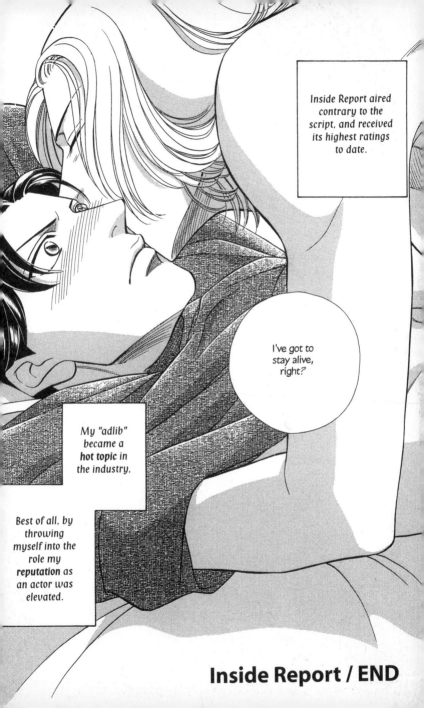

Inside Report aired contrary to the script, and received its highest ratings to date.

I've got to stay alive, right?

My "adlib" became a **hot topic** in the industry.

Best of all, by throwing myself into the role my **reputation** as an actor was elevated.

Inside Report / END

his Best
ヒズベスト

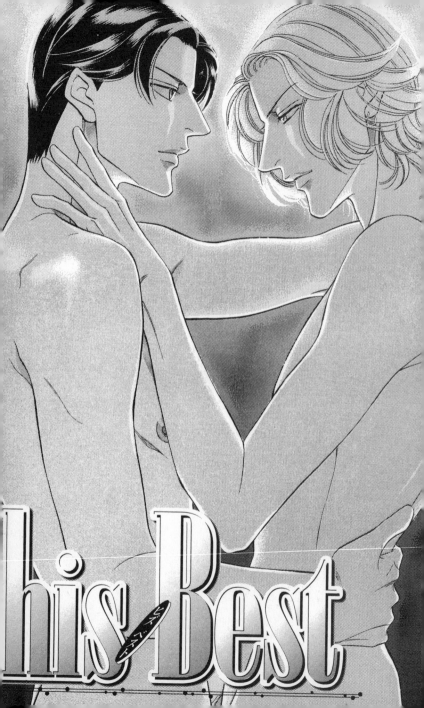

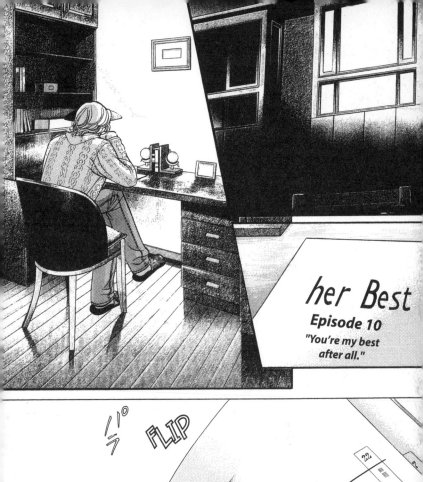

her Best

Episode 10

"You're my best after all."

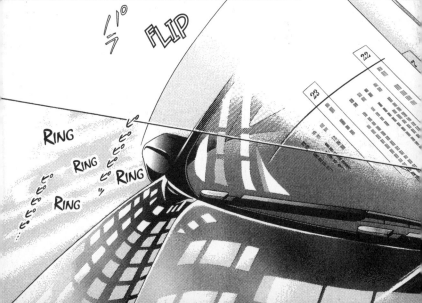

BEEP
Yes?
Is this Iwaki-san?
Sorry to bother you. This is Katou's manager, Kaneko.
Ah! I didn't recognize your number.
You must've gotten mine when Katou and I were working together.
Actually, I have a **message** from Katou...
Well, I guess that **is** the only reason you'd call me.

Where are you now?
Driving home.
I'll be there in about five minutes.
Really? Then you'll be home tonight? Good!
What is it? Is something wrong, Katou?
Actually...No. It's... It's nothing.

Good work today. Goodnight!
Goodnight.
CREAK
キィ

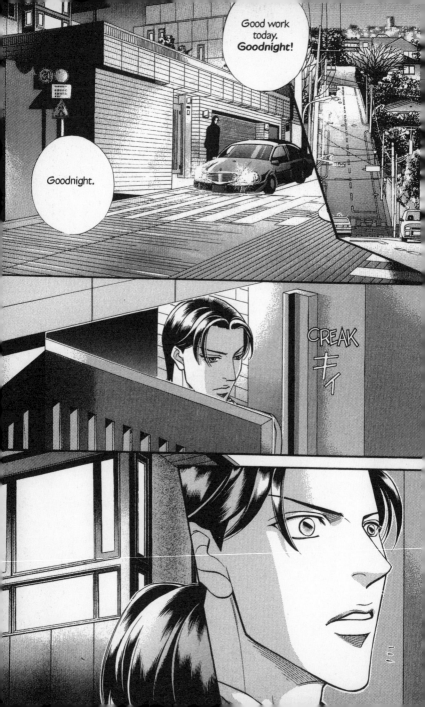

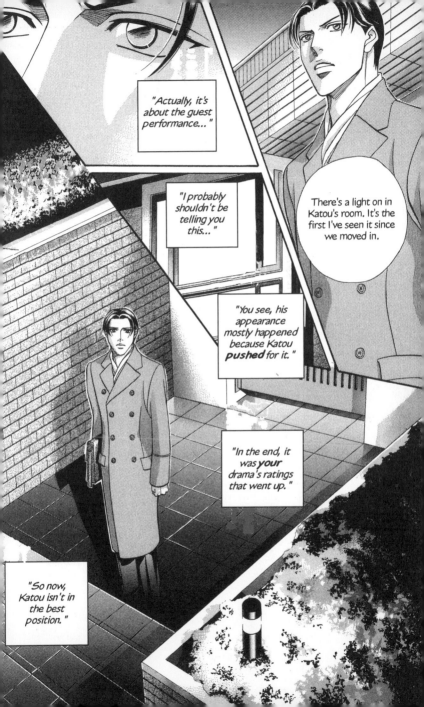

"Actually, it's about the guest performance..."

"I probably shouldn't be telling you this..."

There's a light on in Katou's room. It's the first I've seen it since we moved in.

"You see, his appearance mostly happened because Katou **pushed** for it."

"In the end, it was **your** drama's ratings that went up."

"So now, Katou isn't in the best position."

"Everyone agrees that Katou's performance was marvelous..."
"...And that this role has elevated his status as an actor."
"But his producers were mad since the ratings for Her Best were down."
"It was pretty obvious that he was worried about it today."
"I think he could use your encouragement about now."
ギッ
STRETCH!
"If you could just offer him some kind words..."
KNOCK!
コン
コン
KNOCK!

Katou?
Do you have a minute?
What should I say? It's not like I raised the ratings myself.
K-CHAK
カチャ
I offer me weak uragement ight just his pride.
Welcome home, Iwaki-san.
Are you hungry?
I was going to make something, so if you want...

Really? You **never** cook. Is something wrong?
Is everything **okay?**
All right.
I'll eat.
AGHETTI
Let's enjoy our meal
We still have the soba we got as a housewarming gift.

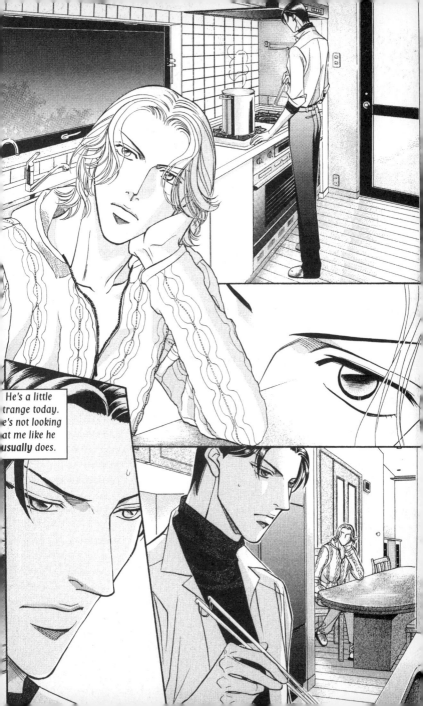

He's a little
strange today.
He's not looking
at me like he
usually does.

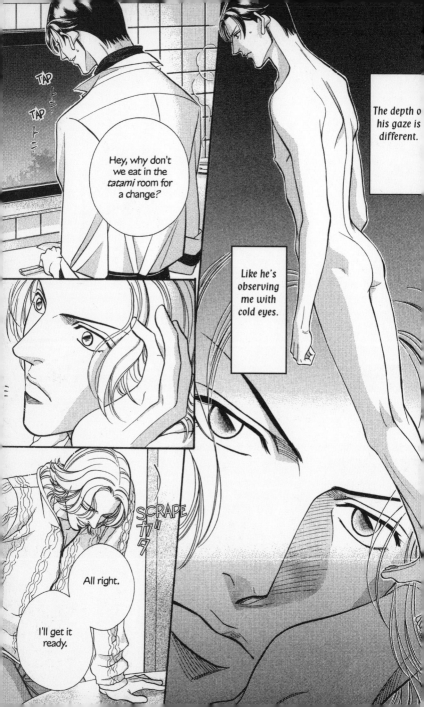

TAP
TAP

Hey, why don't we eat in the *tatami* room for a change?

The depth o his gaze is different.

Like he's observing me with cold eyes.

SCRAPE

All right.

I'll get it ready.

SIGH
ホ…
SLURP
ズズ…
AHEM
ゴホン
ズ…
You're awfully quiet today. Something bothering you?

Hm? Not really.
TMP
カタ
Hmm...not **bothering**, anyway.
I was thinking, I wonder what it is about you that **attracts me.**
TH-THUMP.
ドキ
Huh? What's this all of a sudden?

If it's something in your face...
Or maybe your body that I like.
It's been troubling me.
Troubling...!?
Are you saying you don't know why you love me anymore!?
My face nd body!? Don't be idiculous!!
"If you could just offer him some kind words..."
CLENCH
How should I know?
Hmm. You're right...
Since we're talking about what attracts me.

Since we have this chance, Iwaki-san...
Take off your clothes...
And show me your body.
I want to have sex somewhere brightly lit...
So that I can see properly and **be certain.**

Just kidding.
There's **no way** you'd do that.
STAND
All right.
Wha...!?
Wait...!
I was **joking**, Iwaki-san.

FFUMP
Maybe **you** were kidding, but I'm not!!
If you have some doubt about me...
I'll do **whatever I can** to erase it!!
Then...take everything off and **come here.**

He's looking at me...
Like he's
cking me up...
...With his gaze.

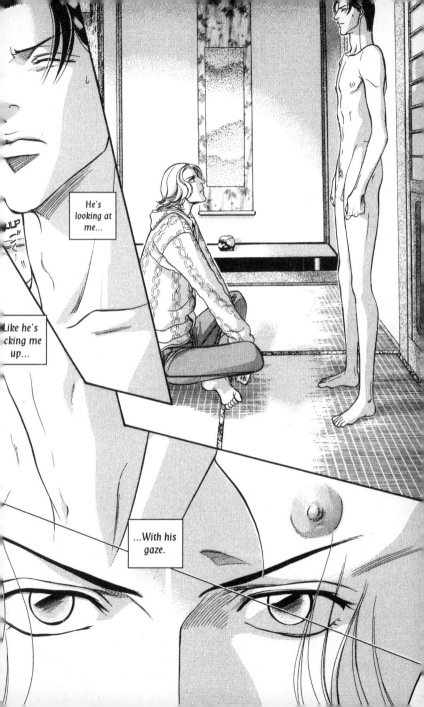

Geez, Iwaki-san.
I see you're feeling **good**, huh?
Ah!
カァ…
BLUSH
Don't hide it.
I won't figure what I **like** about you just by watching.

Ah...?
Aah...!!
You have a beautiful shape...**right here.**
And your legs...

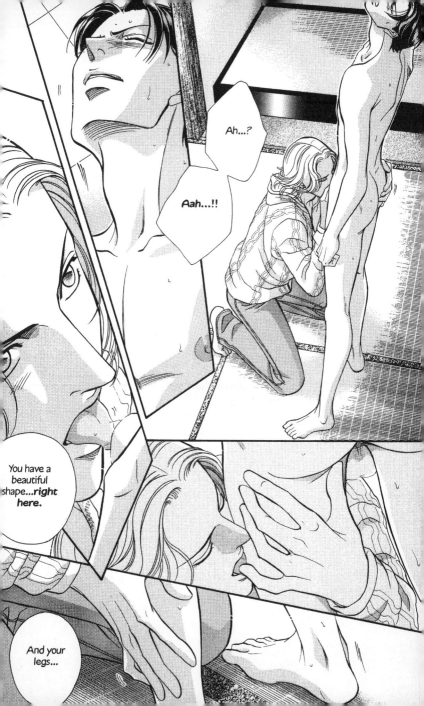

Ungh...
What's wrong? Can't stand?
You're... **different**, today.
This is what Katou was like...when he was still in adult films.
Is it *so* bad...that I'm different?
Why?
You're always the one that puts ***me*** into a trance.
Sometimes it's good to be different, right?

Ahh...
Yes, Katou!
I... I can't take much more! You're... You're so good!
Aah....Yes. Like that, Katou. Just like that!
Glad you like it. Now... I want you to talk dirty to me.

Give it a rest, Katou... Hfff!
Whatever we like about each other, it's not just each other's body!!
I don't want to have sex with you like a porn film!!
If you have something to say, just say it!!
SHIVER
スキン…
I'm sorry. I got carried away.

SQUIKK!
FLINCH
Aahh!!
THAP! THAP!
THAP! THAP!
Un...Ohh!
THAP! THAP!
Katou... Ahh?... Aghh!
THAP! THAP!

...!!
LICK

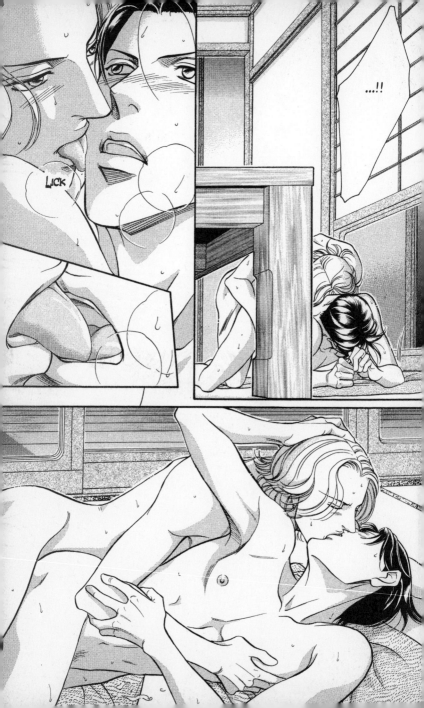

KISS
チュ…
Sorry...I got carried away, thinking we were shooting a porno.
I forgot to watch you properly.
He's too radiant.

Are you **still** not going to tell me why you're **different** today?
Huh? Oh...
Am I **really** that different?
I didn't change when I got home. I was in a working mood.

That's not it!!
You were saying you didn't know why you love me!! I was really hurt!!
Huh!? Ah!!
Is that how you took it!? I'm sorry!!
My drama is called "Her Best," you know!
I have to act as a woman's favorite.
I know the role's characteristics and personality, but I also have to look at myself from the outside.
I started thinking about what it meant to be appealing.
About what a woman is attracted to in a man.

So, since I fell in love with *you*, a *man*...
I had the idea to look you over *as if* I were a *woman.*
Huh?
Are you crazy?
I knew it.
What do you mean!?
You "knew it"!?
Everyone has a preference in what they like about someone.
Ah, you're right!!
So it's no good!
Geez...

He called me...
Saying that you weren't getting along with your staff.
Ah! So that's why you were being so nice to me today!
I guess I was dumb, too, for letting Kaneko's words get to me.
Kaneko?
Why?
The staff and I knew we were risking our ratings, but we didn't think it'd be so much.
I can't even say it was because of me...
Since if it was me people wanted to see, they would've watched my drama.
It's depressing, in a way. My staff thinks so, too.

But it's not so bad thinking to myself, "I'm just getting started!"
It means I **still** have places to go.
Well, whatever the reason, I **dic** strip for you.
So **what part** of me did you like best?
Hmm...It's not that I like guys' **bodies...**

When I fell in love with **you**, I fell in love with **your body.**
Since I love **all of you**, I can't decide on a favorite part.
That's it! What's important is the **person watching!**
If the viewers like **me**, then they'll like my character, too! I don't have to force myself at all!!
...Isn't that what actors without talent do?
That's mean, Iwaki-san!!

his Best/END

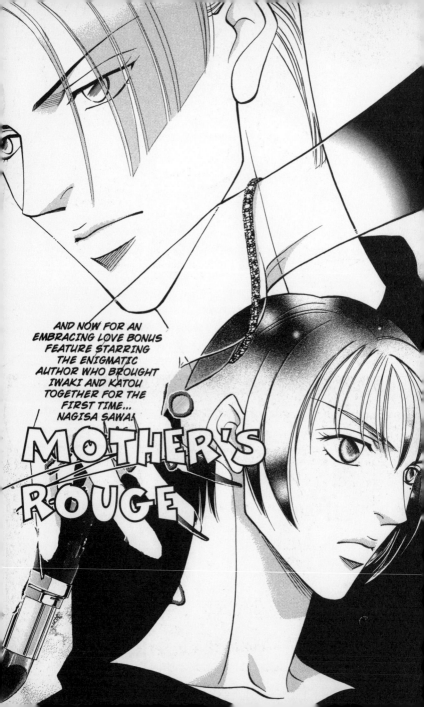

AND NOW FOR AN
EMBRACING LOVE BONUS
FEATURE STARRING
THE ENIGMATIC
AUTHOR WHO BROUGHT
IWAKI AND KATOU
TOGETHER FOR THE
FIRST TIME...
NAGISA SAWA!

MOTHER'S ROUGE

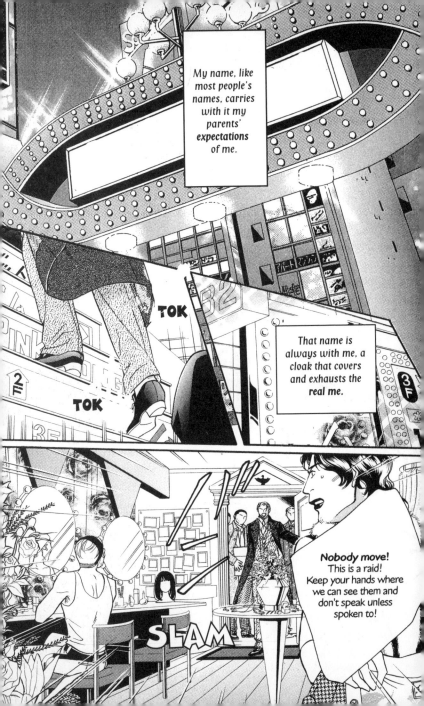

My name, like most people's names, carries with it my parents' expectations of me.

TOK

TOK

That name is always with me, a cloak that covers and exhausts the real me.

SLAM

Nobody move! This is a raid! Keep your hands where we can see them and don't speak unless spoken to!

This building will be searched, under suspicion of illegal drug use!
Nobody move!!
TSUNEO SAWA, TWENTY-THREE YEARS OLD, A DETECTIVE WITH THE CITY POLICE.
The name "Tsuneo" mean "Always behav like a man."
I've always acted so, as to not betray my parents' **expectations.** It became my **belief.**

TH-THUMP!
18
VAMP

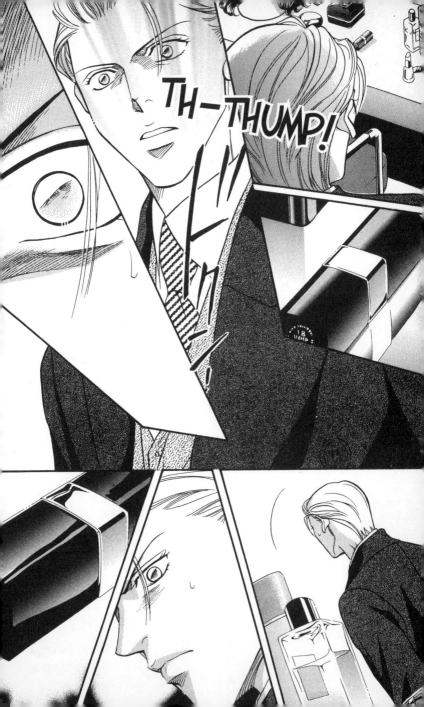

What I didn't know was that my belief...
Was strangling me.
Shinjuku Police Station
Crime Prevention Department
Man, today's arrests were **gross.**
No matter how many times I see ***those people***, I can't get used to it.
uire a vast
he continenta
flected in
tern plains, has
is the "overstretc
the cinemati
EAU

Those guys don't **need** drugs, they're messed up to begin with.
SCRITCH
SCRITCH
SMACK
Hah! No kidding.
Here's my report, Chief.
Ah, good work today.
SLIDE
RUSTLE

It's not for **us** to judge those men... Just because they're ***different***! And no good can ever be had from making idle ***gossip***!
TMP
Remember that everything you say **reflects back** on the entire police department!!
TOK
TOK
WANTED
Fuffff
Just what I'd **expect** to hear from a former bureaucrat.

Sawa's been a complete **pain** ever since he was ***tossed down*** to our district.
Yeah, but his career's not going anywhere with a ***murderer*** in the family.
A certain murder occurred six months ago.
The suspect was caught red-handed. It was a straightforward case...

Yukie!? Yukie!!
The suspect was my uncle-in-law.
The victim was his wife Yukie, age 38.
Oh, Dad, you're home?
Yukihito, call an ambulance!
Your mother won't move!
Yukie!
She died from a wound to her abdomen.
Yukie!!
SPLASH
The crime was discovered by their son, Yukihito Asaki. After reporting his father's crime, Yukie lost his voice. He hasn't spoken since.

They say it was a sudden act, brought on by stress at work and a fight with my aunt.
SAWA
Where's Yukihito?
He's taking a bath.
I guess he still can't eat with us.
He's probably scared of me.
You? Why?
I see fear in his eyes when he looks at me.
His father killed his mother. He's probably scared of men.

Oh? But he gets along fine with Tsuneo.
He probably sees his mother in him.
He looks more like my sister Yukie than either of us.
TMP
Anyway, thanks for dinner.
TUNK
THUNK

Why did I take this?
18 VAMP CHANEL
At the time, I couldn't help but want it... **Desperately.**
Was I **possessed?** Was that it? But why this **lipstick?**
Besides, it's theft! **I committed a crime!**
KNOCK

Come in.
K-CHAK
カチャ
RATTLE
ガタガタ
Yukihito...
What i
ずい
LIFT
NAME OF THE ROSE
Bow
Oh, you finished it already? How about another one?

Why don't we go to the bookstore tomorrow? You'll get **bored** of just my books.
ERA OF LOVE
w that I think of
all my books are
her police related
or love stories.
ERA OF LOVE
GENERATION OF LOVE
SETOUCHI HARUHIKO
How about this for now? It's a little difficult but it's very good.
Do you think it funny that I read these kinds of love stories?
CHUCKLE
SHAKE
SHAKE
eally?

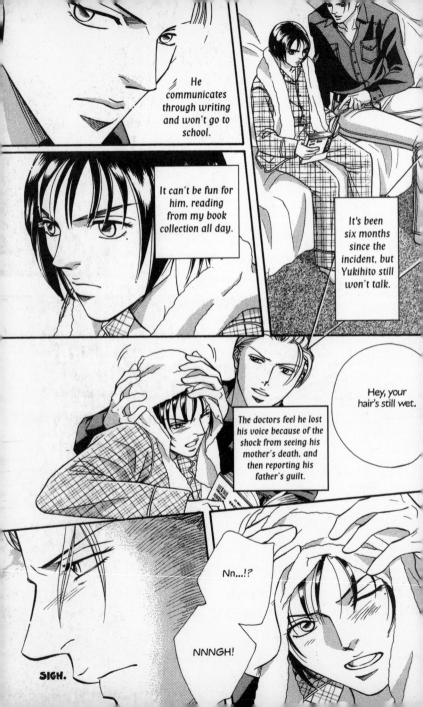

He communicates through writing and won't go to school.

It can't be fun for him, reading from my book collection all day.

It's been six months since the incident, but Yukihito still won't talk.

The doctors feel he lost his voice because of the shock from seeing his mother's death, and then reporting his father's guilt.

Hey, your hair's still wet.

Nn...!?

NNNGH!

SIGH.

ギゅ
HUG
You're so brave...!
KISS

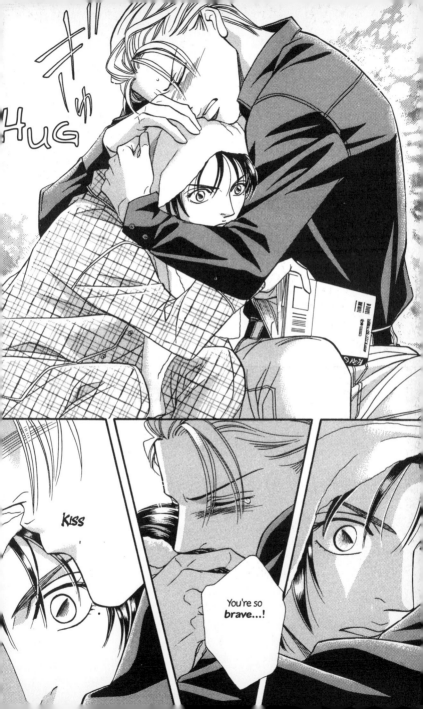

HAH?!
...?
Perhaps it'd be best...For you to go read that in your room.
STAND
K-CHAK

SLAP
What's with me today!?
...Uh...unn!
FSSHT!
FSSHT
What's that sound?

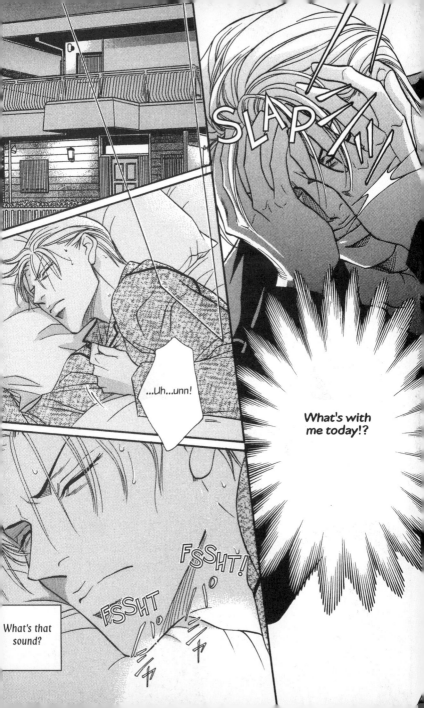

FSSHT!
Lotion?
Who...
Who's that?
CHHP

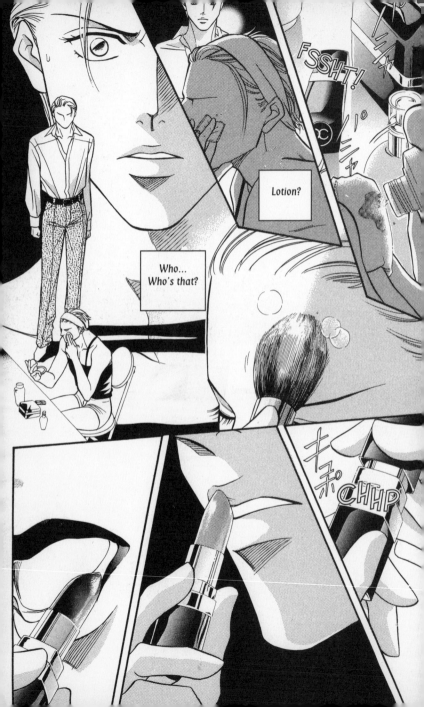

It's...
It's a man!?
T-CHK
Smile
It's...
It's me!!
WHOOSH
No!

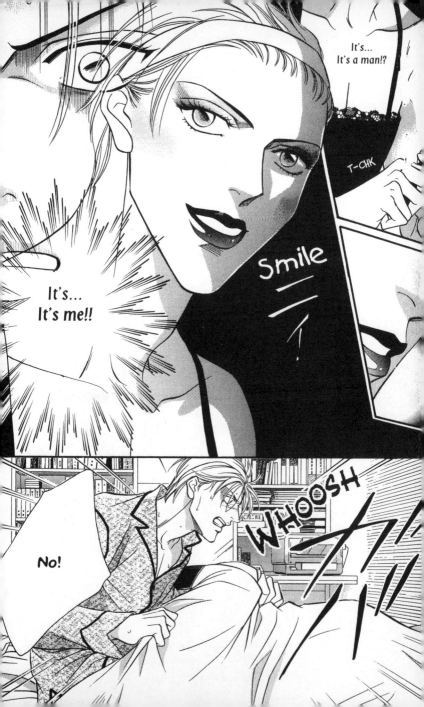

CHIRP
Tremble
Ruffle
HFFFF...
HFFFFF.
I'm...I'm going mad.
Shinjuku Police Station
TAP
How are you importing the drugs!?
.....

Who are you selling the drugs to? Your shop's **customers?**
.....
SIGH
ROLL
Did **you need** the drugs for some reason?
Your shop caters to people with...An ***unusual*** hobby.
By drawing them into our narcotics investigation...
You'll be destroying ***their*** lives as well.
Or was that your **intent** all along?
......

No police officer would understand.
The people that come to my shop aren't all "hobbyists."
TH-THUMP
They were simply born into the wrong gender.
This feeling...agai
The same as when I saw the lipstick.
That feeling that something I want is right in front of me!

Do you think it's easy for a cross-dresser to accept himself!?
Is this what I wish for...?
We're men, yet we feel a sense of satisfaction by dressing as women!
We use the drugs to forget that the world hates us for having the courage to throw off our masculinity!
I would hope... That an officer who truly cares about justice would understand!!
Justice? You might be right.
But I have my conflicts, too.

At your shop yesterday, I acted outside my job as an officer.
I stole...some lipstick. I don't know why. I just had to have it.
Officer...?
I could have just bought some, but I didn't have the courage to accept it... Until now!
But that's not an excuse! No matter what our reasons are...
No matter our justifications!
A crime...
A crime is still a crime! We have to confess to it!

No matter *how ugly* it makes us.

We have to *accept it...*

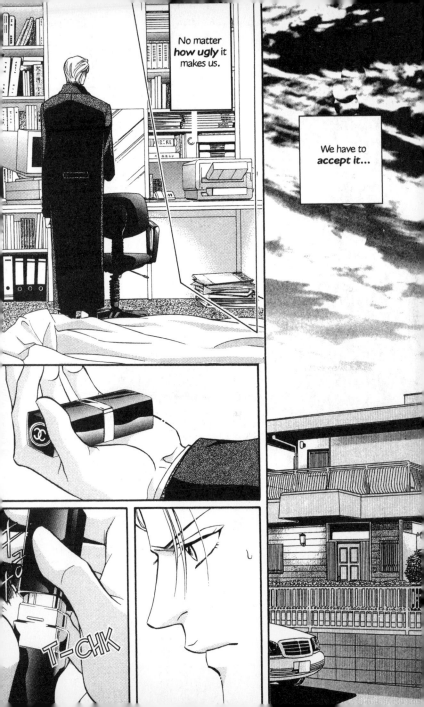

T-CHK

KNOCK
KNOCK
Who?
Tsuneo? You promised to take Yukihito to the bookstore today.
He's been really looking forward...
K-cha
Tsuneo!?

What did you do to your face!?
What are you thinking? Take that make up off!!
RUB
RUB
Take it off right now!!
You look like a FREAK!
You're *so* pathetic!!

Mama...
AH?
DASH
Yukihito?
You...spoke!
Mama!!

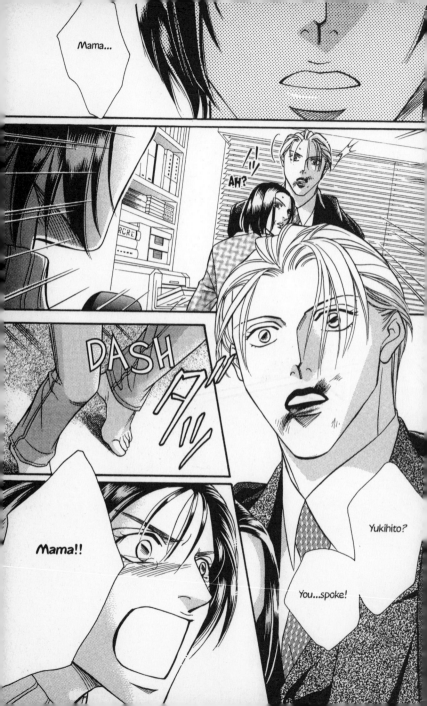

GLOMP
Mama!
Mama!!
Yukihito...
Do you need me...?

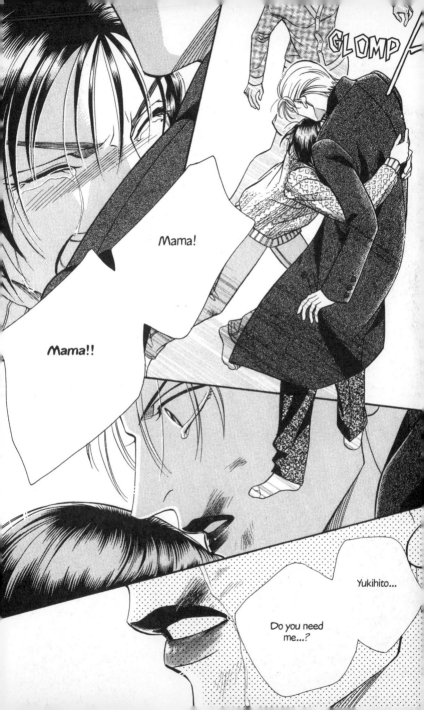

Tsuneo... Did you...? You **pretended** to be Yukie for Yukihito's sake, is that it? **To cure him?!**
That's all you're doing, right? **Right!?**
No.
I'm through with the lying... The **deception.** This is the **real me.**
And there's **something else,** too. Something you should know...
I...I've quit the police force today.

My parents rejected me, and I left home...
But...I'm still your son, Mother! That hasn't changed! Can I still be your son?
REEEEET
...With Yukihito.
GASHON
REEEET
ASHON
Here's the next page, Yukihito.
Somehow, I'm now living as an author.

Is it still to difficult f you? Can y read it?
Nod
I see...
I think one day... I'll write about the people I met as a police officer.
I've seen so many people.
People who love each other, doing work society doesn't accept.

They overcome many conflicts.
What do you think of the title "**Embracing Love**"?
Hmm? **Is that all right?**
Mother's Rouge/END

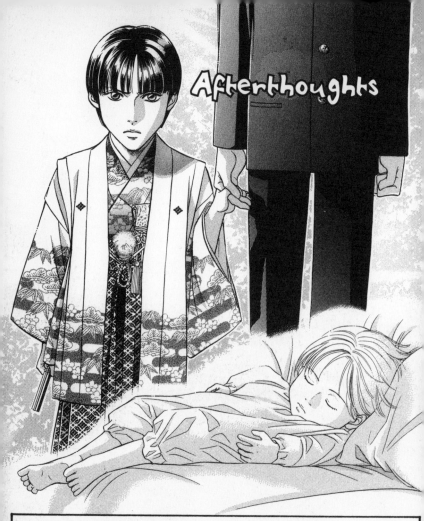

Afterthoughts

On the right is a guest appearance by Iwaki's brother.

Were they really this big when they were born?

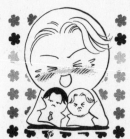

Iwaki and Katou dolls my readers sent me! They're friends!

Volume 4, I'm so happy!

It seems there are people who've been looking forward to these afterthoughts... And Embracing Love.

I'm showing signs of evolution.

I had to mass-produce Katou and Iwaki's face parts (cries)
But along the way I was enjoying the inspiration from struggling through a new job (laugh).
What? I have to draw the insides of their faces!?
And my first experiences with game scenarios and script writing were fun.
Maybe "A Day in the Life of Katou"
Should it be a celebrity simulation or build your own "sweet home life"?
It was my first recording experience, too!
It was my first time working on a song.
Start with AXO!
Amateur
The release for "Gigolo" is coming up as well*.
I was progressing on my work between volume 3 and 4.
*Note: Gigolo is only available in Japan.
VOL 4
STARE
VOL 3
I got this from my readers, too. Katou-dog and Iwaki-dog.
I'm really looking forward to it!
I'm grateful to Biblos for giving me the chance to work outside of manga! I'm waiting for the release myself!
Got a while to go yet.
Not that it has anything to do with it, but I plan to have Yosuke born in the next volume.
By the way, my little sister had a baby recently.
I did this quick drawing for the afterthoughts. Maybe I overdid it?

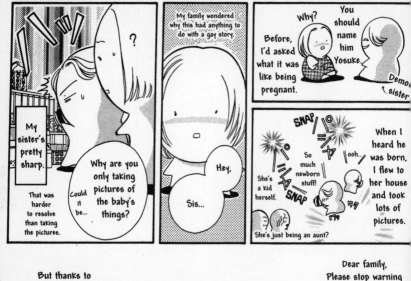

Panel 1:

My sister's pretty sharp.

That was harder to resolve than taking the pictures.

Could it be...

Why are you only taking pictures of the baby's things?

Panel 2:

My family wondered why this had anything to do with a gay story.

Hey,

Sis...

Panel 3:

Before, I'd asked what it was like being pregnant.

Why?

You should name him Yosuke.

Demo sister

Panel 4:

SNAP

So much newborn stuff!

ooh..

She's a kid herself.

SNAP

She's just being an aunt?

When I heard he was born, I flew to her house and took lots of pictures.

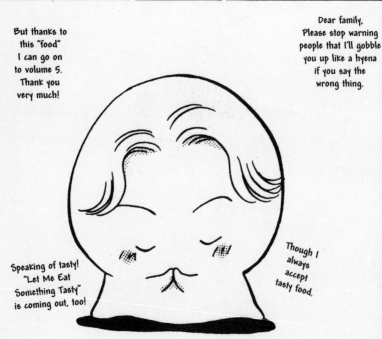

But thanks to this "food" I can go on to volume 5. Thank you very much!

Dear family, Please stop warning people that I'll gobble you up like a hyena if you say the wrong thing.

Speaking of tasty! "Let Me Eat Something Tasty" is coming out, too!

Though I always accept tasty food.

An All-New Romance by the Creator of EMBRACING LOVE

Sound of My Voice

Story & Art by
YOUKA NITTA

Coming
Soon
$15⁹⁹

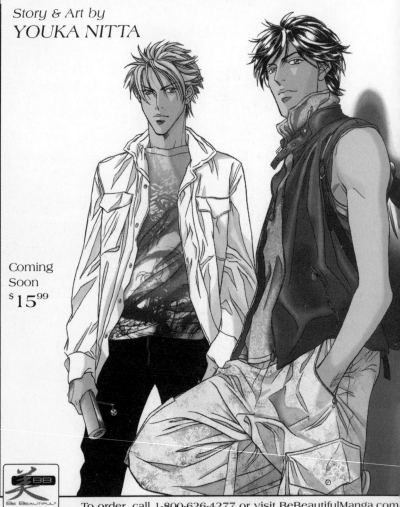

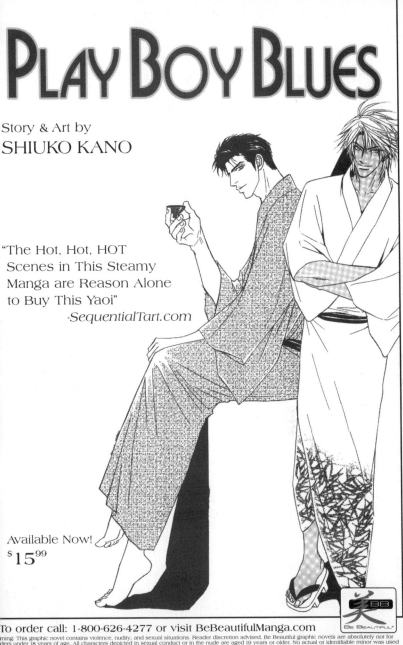

PLAY BOY BLUES

Story & Art by
SHIUKO KANO

"The Hot, Hot, HOT
Scenes in This Steamy
Manga are Reason Alone
to Buy This Yaoi"
         -*SequentialTart.com*

Available Now!
$15⁹⁹

Another Late Night at the Office...

YEBISU
CELEBRITIES

Story by KAORU IWAMOT

Art by SHINRI FUWA

Coming Soon
$15⁹⁹

Coming Soon From Be Beautiful...The Long-Awaited Historical Epic from the Creator of KIZUNA - BONDS OF LOVE

MIDARESOMENISHI

A TALE OF

SAMURAI LOVE

Story & Art by
KAZUMA
KODAKA

$15.99

To order call: 1-800-626-4277 or visit BeBeautifulManga.com

Be Beautiful

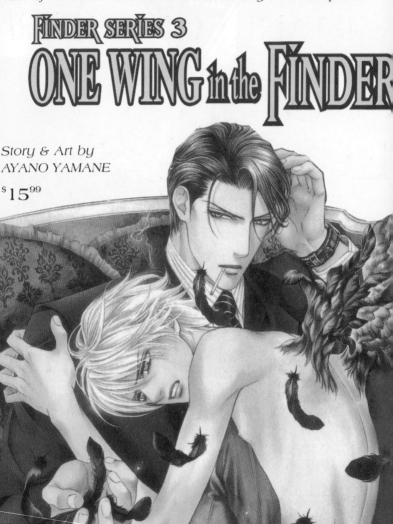

This sign reads "Tomare" and it means:

STOP!

THIS IS THE LAST PAGE OF THE BOOK! DON'T RUIN THE ENDING FOR YOURSELF.

This book is printed in the original Japanese format, which means that it reads from right to left (example on right).

1
2
3
4
5

All Original Yaoi books in our Be Beautiful line are published in his format. The original artwork and sound effects are presented ust like they were in Japan so you can enjoy the comic the way the creators intended.

This format was chosen by YOU, the fans. We conducted a urvey and found that the overwhelming majority of fans prefer their manga in this format.

BB
BE BEAUTIFUL™

The ideogram in the Be Beautiful logo is ronounced as "Be" in Japanese. It means "beauty" or "aestheticism".

ORIGINAL
YAOI™

The ideogram in the Original Yaoi logo is pronounced as "Ai" in Japanese. It means "love".